VERSATILE VEGETABLES

By Katherine Hayes Greenberg and Barbara Kanerva Kyte
Illustrated by Alice Harth

© Copyright 1980
Owlswood Productions, Inc.
1355 Market Street
San Francisco, California 94103

ALL RIGHTS RESERVED
ISBN 0-915942-16-X
First Printing, October 1980
Editor: Susan H. Herbert
Library of Congress Catalogue
Number: 80-83403

TABLE OF CONTENTS

About the Authors 4
Introduction 5
Vegetables Unlimited — from selection to sauces 6
Satisfying Soups and Salads 17
Super Side Dishes 33
Remarkable Main Dishes 45
Recipe Index 62

ABOUT THE AUTHORS

VERSATILE VEGETABLES, the first Owlswood book by cookbook authors Katherine Hayes Greenberg and Barbara Kanerva Kyte, is the result of their life-long acquaintance with garden fresh produce and wholesome homestyle cooking. Katherine grew up on a farm in the Salinas Valley in California where her father produced tomatoes, lettuce, garlic and chile peppers. Barbara spent her first 14 years in the farming region of Minnesota. Now living in Moraga, California with their husbands and children, Katherine and Barbara plant vegetable gardens every summer and harvest the ingredients for their creative vegetable dishes.

INTRODUCTION

Vegetables are a source of wonderful variety. You'll find them available throughout the year in a spectrum of colors, flavors and textures. Whether from a produce market or your own back yard, vegetables please the palate and delight the eye.

VERSATILE VEGETABLES provides nutritious, imaginative and easy-to-follow recipes that help you discover dozens of ways to enjoy vegetables. A simple meal becomes a sumptuous feast with a delicious vegetable side dish. Or let vegetables form the base of your meal's main dish in a casserole, egg dish or stew. Enjoy the elegant versatility of vegetable soups and salads for a quick and tasty lunch, a light first course or a hearty entrée. Also included are special sauces and seasonings to complement vegetables simply yet perfectly prepared.

However you enjoy them, vegetables are easy to use. Here are a few extra suggestions:

- Use fresh vegetables as soon as possible after purchase. If necessary, you can store them in the refrigerator in plastic bags for up to 5 to 7 days. Wash when ready to use.
- Cook vegetables only until just tender to preserve the vitamins and minerals.
- If fresh vegetables are not available, you may substitute frozen (and in some cases canned) vegetables.
- Reserve cooking water for vegetable stocks to be used in soups and casseroles in place of beef or chicken broth.
- Save vegetable leaves and parings for making stock by simmering in water and straining. Freeze stock to have when you want it.
- Purée leftover vegetables in a blender or food processor and add to vegetable stock or chicken broth for soup.
- If you have a sunny window sill, grow your own chives and parsley to snip as needed.

VEGETABLES UNLIMITED...

from selection to sauces

To enjoy the delicious flavors of ripened vegetables, you don't have to go very far—because goodness and nutrition come right from the garden. Use these simple guidelines to select, prepare, cook and serve vegetables at their basic best. Then refer to the sections on Cooking Methods and Sauces later in this chapter.

Artichokes — Select firm green heads with tightly closed leaves. Wash and cut off stem, leaf tips and 1 inch off the top. Rub lemon juice over cut edges. Boil or steam, adding 1 tablespoon olive oil, 1 tablespoon lemon juice, 1 clove garlic and 4 peppercorns to cooking water. Cook for 45 to 60 minutes, or until leaves pull out easily. Serve with Lemon Butter (see page 12), Curried Mayonnaise (see page 14) or Vinaigrette (see page 16).

Asparagus — Select firm green stalks with closed tips. Snap off tough ends and wash. Boil or steam whole for 8 to 10 minutes or cut into 1 inch diagonal slices and stir-fry for 2 minutes. Serve with Hollandaise Sauce (see page 13) or Vinaigrette.

Beets — Select small, firm beets with fresh tops. Cut off roots and stems, peel and slice or shred for soups. Or leave unpeeled and cook, covered, in boiling water for 45 minutes or until tender. Peel, slice and serve with Butter Sauce or in salads with Vinaigrette. Cook beet greens as you do spinach.

Broccoli — Select firm stalks with dark green, tightly closed buds. Remove leaves and tough portions of stalk and wash. Cut large stalks in half. Boil or steam whole for 10 to 12 minutes. Serve with Cheese Sauce (see page 46), or Butter Sauce with Nutmeg (see page 12).

Brussels Sprouts — Select firm green sprouts. Remove outer leaves and trim stems. Wash and boil or steam for 10 to 12 minutes. Serve with Lemon Butter, Vinaigrette or sour cream.

Cabbage — Select firm, crisp heads of green or red cabbage. Remove outer leaves and wash. Shred for cole slaw, salads or soups. Or cut cabbage into wedges and steam for 10 to 15 minutes. Serve hot with Butter Sauce.

Carrots — Select firm, slender carrots. Scrub well and peel if desired. Slice or cut in thin strips. Butter steam for 10 to 15 minutes or stir-fry for 5 minutes. Season with snipped parsley or dill.

Cauliflower — Select compact white heads with fresh green leaves. Remove leaves and core. Wash and boil or steam whole for 20 to 25 minutes or separate into flowerettes and cook for 10 to 12 minutes. Serve with Cheese Sauce or melted butter and Parmesan cheese.

Corn — Select unhusked corn with fresh leaves. The sweetest corn is cooked the day it is picked. Remove husks and silks, wash and boil for 5 to 7 minutes. Serve with butter.

Green Beans — Select slender, crisp green beans. Snap or cut off ends and wash. Leave whole or cut in 1 inch pieces. Boil, steam or butter steam for 10 to 12 minutes. Or stir-fry for 5 minutes. Serve with Garlic Butter Sauce (see page 12), Butter Sauce with toasted sesame seeds or Lemon Butter Sauce seasoned with dill weed.

Mushrooms — Select firm mushrooms with closed caps. Wash gently or wipe with damp paper towel. Trim stems and leave whole or slice. Sauté in melted butter for 3 to 5 minutes. Season with snipped parsley or tarragon.

Onions — Select firm and smooth yellow, white or small boiling onions without sprouts. Remove outer skin and leave whole, slice or chop. Boil or steam until tender and serve with Cheese Sauce. Or add to side dishes, soups, stews and casseroles. Select green onions with fresh green tops to slice into salads or stir-fry with other vegetables. Select firm red onions to slice or chop into salads.

Peas — Select crisp, plump green pods. Shell and wash. Boil or butter steam for 5 minutes. Serve with crushed mint leaves or melted butter.

Peppers — Select firm, smooth dark green or red peppers. Slice off stem end, remove seeds and wash. Leave whole to stuff or slice or chop peppers and stir-fry in 1 tablespoon oil and 1 tablespoon soy sauce with sliced onion. Or add to soups, stews, casseroles or salads.

Potatoes — Select well-shaped, firm potatoes without sprouts or green spots. Idahoes, Russets, sweet potatoes and yams are best for baking. Scrub potatoes, prick skins and bake in 375° or 400° oven for 60 minutes. New and red potatoes are best for boiling. Scrub and boil in their skins for 25 to 35 minutes, or peel and slice and boil for 10 to 15 minutes. Serve with sour cream or Butter Sauce with snipped parsley or chives.

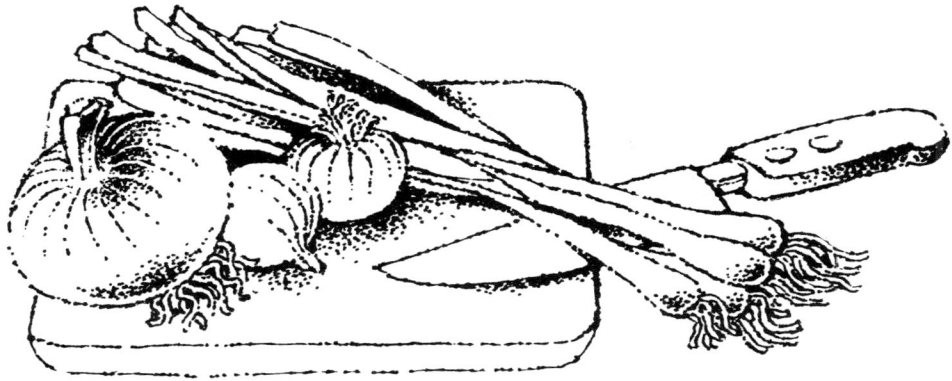

Root Vegetables — Select firm, medium-size celery root, parsnips, rutabagas and turnips. Remove stems and roots, peel and slice. Add to soups or stews. Or cook covered in boiling water for 20 minutes or until tender. Serve with butter.

Spinach — Select crisp, dark green leaves. Remove stems, wash and break up large leaves. Butter steam for 3 to 5 minutes or stir-fry, seasoned with soy sauce, for 2 to 3 minutes.

Summer Squash — Select firm and tender-skinned zucchini, crookneck and pattypan squash. Wash, slice and boil, steam or butter steam for 5 to 8 minutes. Or stir-fry for 3 to 5 minutes. Serve with any one of the Butter Sauce variations.

Swiss chard — Select fresh green leaves. Wash and cut midribs from leaves. Slice midribs and cook in small amount of boiling water for 15 minutes. While midribs are boiling, chop leaves coarsely and add to midribs for last 3 minutes of cooking time. Drain and serve with Butter Sauce or Vinaigrette.

Winter Squash — Select acorn, banana, Hubbard and butternut squash which are heavy for their size. Wash and cut in half or into serving size pieces. Remove seeds and fibers. Brush with melted butter and bake, cut side up, in 375° oven for 50 to 60 minutes. If desired, sprinkle with brown sugar or drizzle with honey before baking.

VEGETABLE COOKING METHODS

Baking — Prick vegetables with a fork and bake in their skins in a 375° oven until tender.

Boiling — Place vegetables in a saucepan with a small amount (1 to 2 inches) of boiling water; cook, covered, until vegetables are just tender.

Butter Steaming — Place 2 tablespoons butter in a saucepan with vegetables and cook, covered, until vegetables are just tender.

Sautéing — Lightly brown vegetables in a scant amount of oil or butter in skillet or saucepan until just tender.

Steaming — Place vegetables on a steaming rack or colander over 1 to 2 inches of boiling water and steam, covered, until just tender.

Stir-frying — Cut vegetables on the diagonal into bite-size, uniform pieces. Heat 1 tablespoon vegetable oil in a Chinese wok or skillet. When oil sizzles, add vegetables and cook, stirring rapidly, until just tender.

To serve au gratin — Combine hot, cooked vegetables with White Sauce (see page 15), sprinkle with bread crumbs or cheese and place under broiler until top is golden brown and crusty.

BUTTER SAUCE
a delicious sauce always just seconds away

1/4 cup butter
optional ingredient (see below)
salt
pepper

In a saucepan, melt butter and stir in any one of the ingredients given below, if desired. Pour sauce over hot cooked vegetables and salt and pepper to taste. Toss lightly and serve immediately.

Optional ingredients:
2 teaspoons lemon juice
1/2 clove garlic, crushed
1 tablespoon chopped parsley or chives
dash oregano, basil, rosemary, dill or nutmeg
1 tablespoon toasted sesame seeds or sliced almonds

HOLLANDAISE SAUCE
serve with asparagus, new potatoes, broccoli or artichokes

1/2 cup butter
2 egg yolks
1 tablespoon hot water
1 tablespoon lemon juice
1/4 teaspoon salt
dash cayenne or nutmeg, optional

Run hot tap water over blender or food processor container to warm. Melt butter and set aside. Place egg yolks, 1 tablespoon hot water, lemon juice, salt and cayenne in blender or food processor and blend. Slowly pour in melted butter, blending until thick. Serve at once. Makes about 3/4 cup.

MAYONNAISE
try this and see how easy it is to make your own

2 egg yolks
2 tablespoons lemon juice or wine vinegar
1/4 teaspoon dry mustard
1/2 teaspoon salt
1-1/3 cups vegetable oil

In a mixing bowl, blender or food processor, combine egg yolks, lemon juice, mustard and salt. While mixing or blending, slowly add oil, mixing until smooth. (If mayonnaise does not thicken, place 2 tablespoons unthickened mayonnaise in a small bowl and beat in 2 teaspoons prepared mustard until thick. Add remaining mayonnaise by teaspoons, mixing until thick after each addition.) Cover and refrigerate up to 2 weeks. Makes about 1-1/2 cups.

Variations — to 1/2 cup of mayonnaise, you may add one of the following:

2 tablespoons minced fresh parsley
2 tablespoons minced fresh chives
2 tablespoons minced fresh watercress
1/4 teaspoon curry powder

Or substitute 2 teaspoons Dijon mustard for dry mustard in recipe and add 2 cloves crushed garlic.

WHITE SAUCE
this versatile sauce is a favorite standby

2 tablespoons butter or margarine
2 tablespoons all-purpose flour
1 cup milk or half and half (light cream)
salt
pepper
optional ingredient (see below)

In a saucepan over low heat, melt butter and add flour, stirring until blended. Remove from heat and add milk, stirring to blend. Return to heat and cook, stirring, until thick and smooth. Add salt and pepper to taste along with any optional ingredient, blending until smooth. Serve immediately. Makes about 1 cup.

Optional ingredients:
dash nutmeg, cayenne, paprika or curry powder
1/4 teaspoon dry mustard, 1/2 teaspoon grated onion and
   1/2 teaspoon Worcestershire sauce
1/4 cup sliced almonds
2 tablespoons capers
1 cup sautéed sliced mushrooms

VINAIGRETTE
delicious tossed with hot or chilled cooked vegetables

3/4 cup olive or peanut oil
1/4 cup wine vinegar
1/4 teaspoon salt
dash pepper
1/2 clove garlic, minced
1 tablespoon capers (optional)
1 tablespoon chopped chives
1/4 teaspoon dry mustard

In a small bowl, combine oil, vinegar, salt, pepper, garlic, capers, chives and mustard. Blend until thoroughly combined. Serve at once or refrigerate for up to 2 weeks. Makes about 1 cup.

SATISFYING SOUPS AND SALADS

ASPARAGUS BISQUE
fresh asparagus makes this a marvelous dinner prelude

2 pounds asparagus, cut in 2 inch lengths
1/4 cup chopped onion
2 cups chicken or vegetable broth
1 teaspoon tarragon
1 cup half and half (light cream)
salt
pepper

In a large saucepan, combine asparagus, onion, broth and tarragon. Bring to boiling, cover and simmer for 10 minutes or until asparagus is tender. Pour into a food processor or blender and blend until smooth. Return to saucepan, stir in cream and salt and pepper to taste. Reheat to serving temperature but *do not boil.* Serves 4.

BORSCHT
top this Russian soup with a spoonful of sour cream and a dash of dill

4 cups beef or vegetable broth
3 beets, peeled and shredded
1 onion, chopped
2 stalks celery, chopped
1-1/2 cups chopped cabbage
2 carrots, shredded
1 potato, shredded

1 (8 oz.) can tomato sauce
1 teaspoon sugar
1 tablespoon vinegar
salt
pepper
sour cream, for garnish
dill weed

In a large saucepan, combine broth, beets, onion, celery, cabbage, carrots, potato, tomato sauce, sugar, vinegar and salt and pepper to taste. Bring to boiling, cover and simmer for 50 minutes or until vegetables are tender. Top each serving with a dollop of sour cream and a sprinkling of dill weed. Serves 6.

CORN CHOWDER
a rich, nutritious soup children will love

1 small onion, chopped
1 small green pepper, chopped
2 stalks celery, chopped
1 tablespoon vegetable oil
2 cups chicken or vegetable broth
2 cups peeled and cubed potatoes
1/4 teaspoon leaf thyme
1 cup half and half (light cream)
2 cups whole corn kernels
salt
pepper

In a saucepan, sauté onion, green pepper and celery in hot oil until soft but not browned. Add broth, potatoes and thyme. Bring to a boil, cover and simmer for 15 minutes or until potatoes are tender. Add cream, corn and salt and pepper to taste. Reheat to serving temperature but *do not boil*. Serves 4 to 6.

CREAM OF BROCCOLI SOUP
accompany this with a sandwich for a satisfying lunch

5 cups chopped broccoli (about 1 large bunch)
1/2 cup chopped onion
2 cups chicken or vegetable broth
1-1/2 cups half and half (light cream)
salt
pepper

In a saucepan, combine broccoli, onion and broth. Bring to boiling, cover and simmer for 10 minutes or until broccoli is tender. Place in food processor or blender and blend until smooth. Return to saucepan, stir in cream and salt and pepper to taste. Reheat to serving temperature but *do not boil*. Serves 4.

MINESTRONE
a vegetable laden soup to serve with crusty garlic bread

1/2 cup small white beans
2 cups water
4 cups chicken or vegetable broth
1 clove garlic, minced
1 cup shredded cabbage
1/2 cup chopped onion
2 carrots, sliced
1 potato, cubed
1 (16 oz.) can tomatoes, chopped, and their liquid
1 stalk celery, chopped
1 zucchini, sliced
1/4 cup chopped fresh parsley
1 teaspoon basil
1/2 teaspoon marjoram
1/2 cup broken spaghetti
salt
pepper
grated Parmesan cheese

Rinse beans and soak in 2 cups water overnight; *or* bring water and beans to a boil, cook for 2 minutes, remove from heat and let stand, covered, for 1 hour. Add broth, garlic, cabbage, onion, carrots, potato, tomatoes and their liquid, celery, zucchini, parsley, basil, marjoram, spaghetti and salt and pepper to taste. Bring to a boil, cover and simmer for 45 minutes or until beans are tender. Garnish each serving with Parmesan cheese. Serves 6 to 8.

MUSHROOM BARLEY SOUP
a hearty thick soup for mushroom lovers

4 cups beef or vegetable broth
1/2 cup pearl barley
1/2 pound fresh mushrooms, sliced
1 small onion, chopped
1 small green pepper, chopped
3 tablespoons butter or margarine
3 tablespoons all-purpose flour
1 cup milk
1/4 cup chopped fresh parsley
salt
pepper

In a large saucepan, bring broth to a boil and add barley. Cover and simmer for 45 minutes. Meanwhile, in a large skillet, sauté mushrooms, onion and green pepper in butter until tender. Stir in flour. Add milk, stirring until thickened. Add mushroom mixture to barley with parsley and salt and pepper to taste. Simmer 15 minutes or until barley is tender. Serves 4 to 6.

POTATO, LEEK AND SPINACH SOUP
an attractive, flavorful soup to begin a special dinner

2 leeks, sliced*
3 medium-size potatoes, peeled and cubed
4 cups chicken or vegetable broth
3 cups chopped spinach, loosely packed
1 cup half and half (light cream)
salt
pepper

In a large saucepan, combine leeks, potatoes and broth. Bring to a boil, cover and simmer for 25 minutes or until potatoes are tender. Add spinach and simmer 5 minutes longer. Place in food processor or blender and blend until smooth. Return to saucepan and stir in cream and salt and pepper to taste. Reheat to serving temperature but *do not boil.* Serves 4 to 6.

*To clean leeks thoroughly, cut lengthwise to expose center of stalk. Rinse layers well as needed.

TOMATO SOUP
top this irresistible homemade version with Parmesan cheese

1 tablespoon vegetable oil
1 onion, chopped
1 clove garlic, minced
4 cups chopped tomatoes
1 cup chicken or vegetable broth
1 tablespoon fresh coriander or parsley
salt
pepper
grated Parmesan cheese

In a large saucepan, heat oil and sauté onion and garlic until onion is tender. Add tomatoes, broth, coriander and salt and pepper to taste. Bring to boiling, cover and simmer for 15 minutes. Place in a food processor or blender and blend until smooth. Return to saucepan to reheat to serving temperature. Sprinkle each serving with Parmesan cheese. Serves 6.

VEGETABLE SOUP
rediscover the wholesomeness of this old-fashioned soup

2 tablespoons butter or margarine
1/2 cup chopped onion
2 stalks celery, sliced
2 carrots, sliced
1 turnip, cubed
1 potato, cubed
4 cups chicken or vegetable broth
2 tablespoons chopped fresh parsley
salt
pepper
1 cup green peas

In a saucepan, melt butter and sauté onion and celery until tender. Add carrots, turnip, potato, broth, parsley and salt and pepper to taste. Bring to a boil, cover and simmer for 30 minutes or until vegetables are tender. Add peas and cook 5 minutes longer. Serves 6.

WINTER SQUASH SOUP
an unusual, creamy soup with a hint of nutmeg

2 tablespoons butter or margarine
1/4 cup chopped onion
2 tablespoons all-purpose flour
1/4 teaspoon nutmeg
2 cups chicken or vegetable broth
1 cup cooked cubed acorn, banana, Hubbard or butternut squash or pumpkin
1/2 cup half and half (light cream)
salt
pepper
chopped fresh parsley, for garnish

In a saucepan, melt butter and sauté onion until tender. Stir in flour and nutmeg. Slowly pour in broth, stirring constantly. Bring to a boil and add squash. Return to boiling, cover and simmer 5 minutes. Place in food processor or blender and blend until smooth. Return to saucepan and stir in cream and salt and pepper to taste. Reheat to serving temperature but *do not boil*. Garnish with parsley. Serves 4.

ZUCCHINI SOUP

a simply delicious soup that's ready in no time at all

2 tablespoons butter or margarine
1 onion, chopped
2 cloves garlic, minced
1 pound zucchini, sliced
2 tablespoons chopped fresh parsley
1 teaspoon basil
3 cups chicken or vegetable broth
salt
pepper
seasoned croutons, for garnish

In a saucepan, melt butter and sauté onion and garlic until onion is tender. Add zucchini, parsley, basil, broth and salt and pepper to taste. Bring to a boil, cover and simmer for 15 minutes or until vegetables are tender. Place in food processor or blender and blend until smooth. Return to saucepan to reheat to serving temperature, if necessary. Garnish each serving with seasoned croutons. Serves 4.

NICOISE SALAD
make this your choice for a satisfying, eye-appealing entrée

2/3 cup olive oil
1/3 cup lemon juice or white wine vinegar
1 teaspoon Dijon mustard
1/4 teaspoon salt
dash freshly ground pepper
2 potatoes, cooked, peeled and sliced
2 cups green beans, cooked tender-crisp
lettuce leaves
1 cup cherry tomatoes
4 hard-cooked eggs, quartered
4 slices red onion, separated into rings
1/2 cup ripe pitted olives
2 tablespoons capers
2 tablespoons minced fresh parsley

To make dressing, combine oil, lemon juice, mustard, salt and pepper in a small bowl. Place potatoes and green beans in separate bowls and pour 1/4 cup dressing over each. Set aside. Arrange lettuce leaves among 4 dinner plates and arrange tomatoes, eggs, onion rings, olives, beans and potatoes attractively on lettuce. Sprinkle each serving with capers, parsley and remaining dressing. Serves 4.

TOSSED GREENS WITH CONFETTI DRESSING
this colorful vegetable dressing makes any salad a celebration

3/4 cup sour cream
1 teaspoon lemon juice
dash salt
dash pepper
2 tablespoons chopped radishes
2 tablespoons shredded carrots
1 green onion, thinly sliced
1 bunch spinach or head lettuce, torn into pieces

In a small bowl, combine sour cream, lemon juice, salt, pepper, radishes, carrots and green onion. Cover and chill (up to 24 hours) until ready to serve. Just before serving, pour over spinach and toss. Makes about 1 cup dressing.

GAZPACHO SALAD
a refreshing summer salad garnished with sour cream

2 (12 oz.) cans tomato juice
2 envelopes unflavored gelatin
1/4 cup red wine vinegar
1/4 teaspoon salt
dash pepper
dash Tabasco sauce
2 tomatoes, seeded and chopped
1 cup minced cucumber
1 cup minced green pepper
1/4 cup minced onion
1/4 cup chopped fresh parsley
lettuce leaves
sour cream, for garnish

Pour 1 can tomato juice in saucepan and place over low heat. Add gelatin, stirring constantly until dissolved. Remove from heat and add vinegar, salt, pepper, Tabasco sauce and remaining tomato juice. Chill until partially set. Fold in tomatoes, cucumber, green pepper, onion and parsley. Pour into 6 cup ring mold and chill until firm. Unmold onto a plate of lettuce leaves and add a dollop of sour cream to each serving. Serves 6.

TOMATOES WITH AVOCADO DRESSING
a rich dressing tops ripe red tomatoes

1 ripe avocado, peeled and pitted
1/4 cup mayonnaise
1 tablespoon lemon juice
dash Worcestershire sauce
dash salt
lettuce leaves
4 tomatoes, sliced
1/2 red onion, thinly sliced and separated into rings

In a food processor or blender, place avocado, mayonnaise, lemon juice, Worcestershire sauce and salt; blend until smooth. Arrange lettuce leaves on 4 salad plates and arrange tomato slices and onion rings on lettuce. Pour avocado dressing over all. Serves 4.

CRUDITES WITH PESTO DIP
when fresh basil is unavailable, substitute fresh parsley

1 egg
1 clove garlic, peeled
1 tablespoon wine vinegar
1/4 cup fresh basil leaves *or* 1/4 cup fresh parsley leaves with
    1/2 teaspoon dried basil
1/4 teaspoon salt
dash pepper
1/4 cup grated Parmesan cheese
1/2 cup olive oil
Assorted fresh vegetables:
    cucumber, celery, carrot and zucchini sticks
    strips of green or red pepper
    cauliflower and broccoli flowerettes
    mushrooms and cherry tomatoes

In a food processor or blender, place egg, garlic, vinegar, basil, salt, pepper and Parmesan cheese. Blend until smooth. Continuing to blend, add oil in a thin stream. Refrigerate (up to 12 hours) until ready to use. Serve surrounded with an assortment of prepared fresh vegetables. Makes about 1 cup dressing.

SUPER SIDE DISHES

TANGY ARTICHOKES
serve piping hot or make ahead and serve chilled

4 artichokes
1 tablespoon lemon juice or vinegar
1/4 cup olive oil
3 tablespoons white wine vinegar
1/4 teaspoon dry mustard
1 teaspoon Worcestershire sauce
1 clove garlic, crushed
salt
pepper

Cut stems off artichokes and remove tough outer leaves. Trim tips off leaves. Place artichokes in saucepan or steamer with 2 inches of water. Add lemon juice to water, cover and cook 45 to 60 minutes or until leaves pull out easily. Meanwhile, in a small bowl, combine olive oil, vinegar, mustard, Worcestershire sauce, garlic and salt and pepper to taste. Place cooked artichokes in serving dish and pour dressing over all. Serves 4.

ASPARAGUS POLANAISE
enjoy this traditional way to serve tender asparagus

2 pounds fresh asparagus
1/4 cup dry bread crumbs
2 tablespoons butter or margarine
1 hard-cooked egg, finely chopped

Snap tough ends off asparagus spears. Boil or steam asparagus until just tender, about 8 to 10 minutes. Remove to serving platter and keep warm. In a small pan, sauté bread crumbs in butter until lightly browned. Sprinkle crumbs over asparagus. Garnish with egg. Serves 4.

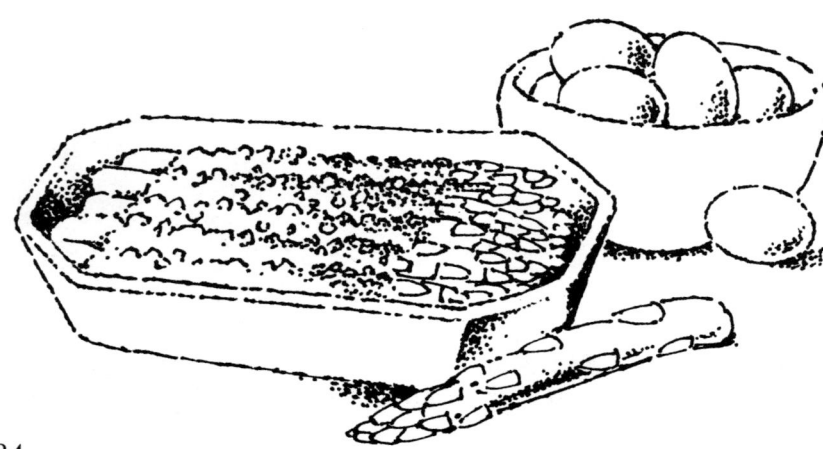

SESAME BROCCOLI FLOWERETTES
toasted sesame seeds add a unique crunch to this dish

4 cups broccoli flowerettes
2 tablespoons butter or margarine
2 teaspoons lemon juice
1/2 teaspoon grated lemon peel
1 tablespoon sesame seeds, toasted as directed below

Boil or steam broccoli flowerettes until just tender, about 6 to 8 minutes. Drain and place on serving platter. Add butter, lemon juice, lemon peel and toasted sesame seeds. Toss and serve at once. Serves 4.

To toast sesame seeds, place seeds in a small skillet over low heat. Cook, stirring occasionally, until lightly browned.

BRUSSELS SPROUTS PARMESAN
enjoy this special treatment for Brussels sprouts

3 cups Brussels sprouts
2 tablespoons melted butter or margarine
1 teaspoon lemon juice
salt
pepper
1/4 cup grated Parmesan cheese

Cut stems off sprouts and remove outer leaves. Steam or boil sprouts for 10 minutes or until just tender. Drain and place sprouts in baking dish. Combine butter with lemon juice and salt and pepper to taste; pour butter mixture over sprouts and sprinkle with Parmesan cheese. Bake in 350° oven for 15 minutes. Serves 4.

ORANGE GLAZED CARROTS AND ONIONS
simmered in a sauce with a hint of honey

3 cups carrots, cut in 1 inch slices
8 small whole white onions, peeled
1 tablespoon butter or margarine
2 tablespoons orange juice
1 tablespoon honey
dash salt

Place carrots and onions in a large saucepan with butter, orange juice, honey and salt. Bring to a boil, cover and reduce heat. Simmer for 25 minutes or until carrots and onions are tender. Serves 4 to 6.

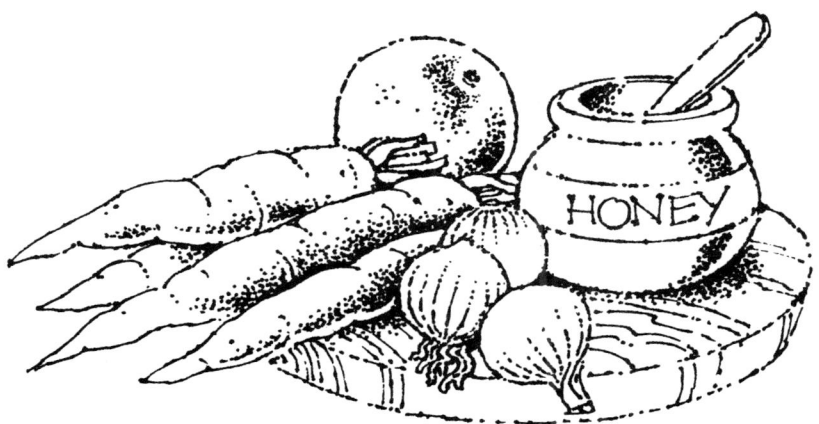

FRENCH FRIED EGGPLANT
make these "french fries" from tender eggplant

1 eggplant, peeled
3/4 to 1 cup dry bread crumbs
2 eggs, beaten
3/4 to 1 cup vegetable oil
salt
grated Parmesan cheese

Slice eggplant lengthwise into 1/2 by 1/2 inch strips. Place 3/4 cup crumbs in a paper or plastic bag. Dip each eggplant strip in eggs and then shake in bag to coat with crumbs. Continue until all strips are coated, adding more crumbs to bag as needed. In a large skillet, heat 3/4 cup oil to 375° and fry eggplant, in several batches, until golden brown. Drain on paper towels and continue until all are cooked, adding more oil as needed. Sprinkle with salt and Parmesan cheese. Serves 4 to 6.

CHEESE POTATOES
a rich and cheese-filled side dish to accompany meats

3 medium-size potatoes
2 cups shredded cheddar cheese
1/2 cup sour cream
2 tablespoons chopped onion
salt
pepper

In a saucepan, boil unpeeled potatoes for about 15 minutes, or until they just begin to soften. Peel and grate potatoes. Set aside. In a large bowl, combine cheese, sour cream, onion and salt and pepper to taste. Stir in potato. Spoon mixture into a greased baking dish and bake in a 350° oven for 30 minutes or until heated through and top is crusty. Serves 4.

POTATO PANCAKES
delicious served hot with apple sauce or sour cream

4 potatoes, peeled, grated and drained
1 small onion, grated
1/2 teaspoon salt
1/2 teaspoon baking powder
2 tablespoons all-purpose flour
2 eggs, beaten
vegetable oil

In a large bowl, mix together potatoes, onion, salt, baking powder, flour and eggs. Pour vegetable oil to a depth of 1/4 inch in a large skillet. Heat oil and add potato mixture by spoonfuls. Fry on both sides until golden brown and drain briefly on paper towels. Place on baking sheet and bake in 350° oven for 10 minutes. Serves 4.

SUCCOTASH
the Colonists enjoyed the combination of corn and lima beans

1-1/2 cups whole corn kernels
1-1/2 cups cooked lima beans
dash salt
1/2 cup boiling water
1/2 cup sour cream
paprika (optional)

In a saucepan, combine corn, lima beans and salt with boiling water. Cover and cook for 5 minutes. Drain and stir in sour cream. Sprinkle with paprika, if desired. Serves 4.

SHERRIED SWEET POTATOES
a superb choice for your holiday dinner

4 sweet potatoes or yams
2 tablespoons butter or margarine
1/4 cup brown sugar
3 tablespoons sherry
1/2 cup chopped pecans

Boil potatoes in their skins for 20 minutes or until tender. Drain and peel. In a large bowl, mash potatoes with butter and mix in sugar and sherry. Place in greased baking dish and sprinkle with pecans. Bake in 350° oven for 30 minutes or until hot and bubbly. Serves 4 to 6.

STUFFED ZUCCHINI
a hint of dill complements the cream cheese filling

4 small zucchini
3 ounces cream cheese, softened at room temperature
1 green onion, sliced
dash salt
dash cayenne
1/2 cup sour cream
dill weed

Boil whole zucchini 5 minutes or until just beginning to soften. Cool slightly, cut in half lengthwise and carefully scoop out seeds. Place shells on baking sheet and set aside. In a small bowl, combine seeds with cream cheese, green onion, salt and cayenne. Spoon mixture into zucchini shells. Top with sour cream and sprinkle with dill. Bake in 350° oven for 10 minutes. Serves 4 to 6.

ORIENTAL STYLE SPINACH
a quick and tasty way to serve this nutritious vegetable

2 bunches spinach, stems removed
1 tablespoon vegetable oil
1 tablespoon soy sauce
1 green onion, sliced
1/2 cup sliced water chestnuts

Tear spinach leaves into 2 inch pieces. Heat oil and soy sauce in wok or skillet. Add spinach, green onion and water chestnuts. Cook, covered, for 2 minutes or until spinach is wilted. Uncover and cook, stirring, 1 minute longer. Serves 4.

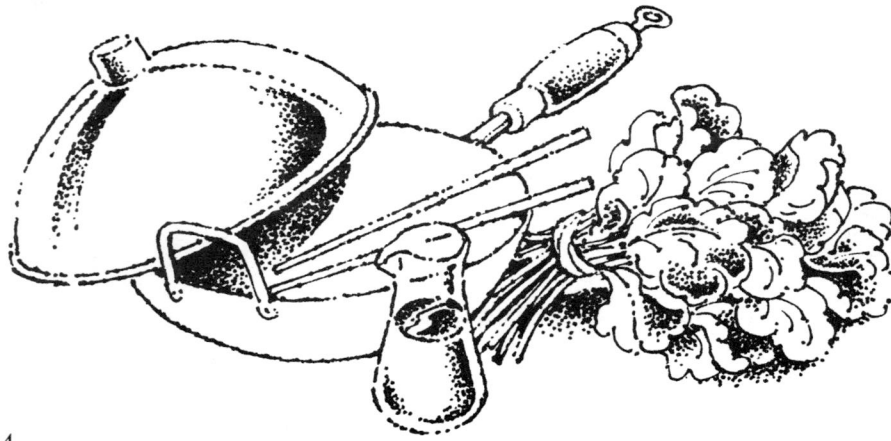

REMARKABLE MAIN DISHES

ARTICHOKE QUICHE
baked in a tender crust of fresh, sautéed mushrooms

1/2 pound fresh mushrooms, chopped
2 tablespoons butter or margarine
1/4 cup dry bread crumbs
3 eggs, beaten
1/2 cup milk
1-1/2 cups shredded cheddar cheese
1 (6 oz.) jar marinated artichoke hearts, drained and chopped
    or 1 cup chopped artichoke hearts
1/2 teaspoon oregano (optional)

In a small skillet, sauté mushrooms in butter until tender. Stir in bread crumbs. Press mushroom mixture into the bottom of a greased 9 inch pie plate. In a medium-size bowl, combine eggs, milk, cheese, artichokes and oregano. Pour over mushrooms and bake in a 350° oven for 40 minutes or until a knife inserted in the center comes out clean. Serves 4.

BROCCOLI SOUFFLE
a richly golden crust makes this an elegant luncheon favorite

2 cups chopped broccoli
2 tablespoons butter or margarine
2 tablespoons all-purpose flour
1/2 cup milk
1/4 teaspoon nutmeg

1/4 teaspoon salt
dash pepper
4 egg yolks
4 egg whites, beaten until stiff
Cheese Sauce (recipe follows)

Steam or boil broccoli for 5 minutes or until tender. Drain and set aside. In a saucepan, melt butter and blend in flour. Add milk gradually and cook, stirring, until thickened. Stir in nutmeg, salt, pepper and broccoli. In a large bowl, beat egg yolks; mix in broccoli mixture. Fold in egg whites. Pour into a greased 1-1/2 quart soufflé dish. Bake in 350° oven for 30 minutes or until a knife inserted into the center comes out clean. Spoon hot Cheese Sauce over each serving. Serves 4 to 6.

To make Cheese Sauce, melt 1 tablespoon butter or margarine in a small saucepan and stir in 1 tablespoon all-purpose flour until blended. Slowly pour in 1/2 cup milk, stirring until thickened. Stir in 1/2 cup shredded cheddar cheese, 1/4 teaspoon Worcestershire sauce and salt and pepper to taste. Makes about 3/4 cup.

CARROT RICE CASSEROLE
a savory blend of carrots, rice and Swiss cheese

2 tablespoons chopped onion
1 tablespoon butter or margarine
2 cups shredded carrots
1 cup cooked rice
3 eggs, beaten
1/4 teaspoon salt
dash pepper
1 cup shredded Swiss cheese

In a saucepan, sauté onion in butter until tender. Allow to cool slightly. Stir in carrots, rice, eggs, salt, pepper and Swiss cheese. Spoon mixture into a greased baking dish and bake, covered, in a 350° oven for 30 minutes or until hot and bubbly. Serves 4.

CAULIFLOWER AND WALNUT CASSEROLE
walnuts add a distinctive texture to this light entrée

1 medium-size head cauliflower, cut into flowerettes
1 cup sour cream
1 cup shredded cheddar cheese
1/4 teaspoon dry mustard
1/3 cup chopped walnuts
3 tablespoons dry bread crumbs

Steam or boil cauliflower for 10 minutes or until just tender. Drain. In a mixing bowl, combine cauliflower with sour cream, cheese and mustard. Spoon into a greased baking dish. Combine walnuts with bread crumbs and sprinkle over cauliflower. Bake in a 350° oven for 20 minutes or until hot and bubbly. Serves 4.

CRACKED WHEAT CABBAGE ROLLS
a delightfully textured filling wrapped in tender cabbage leaves

6 large cabbage leaves
1/4 cup chopped onion
1/2 cup chopped carrot
2 tablespoons butter or margarine
3/4 cup cracked wheat bulgar
2 tablespoons chopped fresh parsley
dash salt
dash pepper
1-1/2 cups chicken or vegetable broth
1 (15 oz.) can tomato sauce
1/4 teaspoon savory

Parboil or steam cabbage leaves for 5 minutes. Drain and set aside. In a saucepan, sauté onion and carrot in butter until tender. Stir in bulgar, parsley, salt, pepper and broth. Bring to boiling, reduce heat and simmer, covered, for 15 minutes or until liquid is absorbed. Spoon bulgar mixture on cabbage leaves, wrap into bundles and place side by side in a greased baking dish. In a small bowl, combine tomato sauce with savory and pour mixture over cabbage. Bake in 350° oven for 45 minutes or until sauce is bubbly. Serves 4 to 6.

CHILE CORN CASSEROLE
the flavors of Mexico are captured in this zippy casserole

2 eggs, beaten
1 cup sour cream
2 cups whole corn kernels
1 (4 oz.) can chopped green chiles
1/2 cup yellow cornmeal
1/2 teaspoon salt
2 cups shredded Monterey jack or cheddar cheese

In a large bowl, combine eggs, sour cream, corn, chiles, cornmeal, salt and cheese. Spoon mixture into a greased baking dish and bake at 350° for 40 minutes or until a knife inserted into the center comes out clean. Serves 4 to 6.

EGGPLANT PARMIGIANA
a continental favorite you'll enjoy often

1/2 cup chopped onion
1 clove garlic, minced
3 tablespoons olive oil
1 (16 oz.) can tomatoes, chopped, and their liquid
2 tablespoons tomato paste or catsup
1/2 teaspoon oregano
1/2 teaspoon basil

dash salt
dash pepper
1/2 cup dry bread crumbs
grated Parmesan cheese
1 eggplant, cut into 1/4 inch slices
2 eggs, beaten
8 ounces Mozzarella cheese, shredded

In a saucepan, sauté onion and garlic in 1 tablespoon oil until tender. Add tomatoes, their liquid, tomato paste, oregano, basil, salt and pepper. Bring to a boil, reduce heat and simmer for 30 minutes. Combine bread crumbs with 1/2 cup Parmesan cheese. Set aside. Dip eggplant slices into beaten eggs, then coat with crumb mixture. Sauté eggplant on both sides in 2 tablespoons olive oil until golden brown. In a greased baking dish, make a layer of half of the eggplant; top with half of the tomato sauce and half of the Mozzarella cheese. Repeat layers and sprinkle with Parmesan cheese. Bake in 350° oven for 30 minutes or until hot. Serves 6.

SPANISH OMELET

served with a salad, this makes a quick, light meal

1/4 cup chopped onion
1/4 cup chopped green pepper
1 clove garlic minced
1 cup sliced fresh mushrooms
1 tablespoon vegetable oil
1 (8 oz.) can tomato sauce
1/2 teaspoon basil
salt
pepper
8 eggs, beaten
1/4 cup milk
1 tablespoon butter or margarine

In a skillet, sauté onion, green pepper, garlic and mushrooms in oil until just tender. Stir in tomato sauce, basil and salt and pepper to taste. Simmer 15 minutes. Meanwhile, in a mixing bowl, beat together eggs, milk and a dash of salt and pepper. In another skillet, melt butter and pour in eggs. Cook slowly, lifting up edge of omelet with spatula to let uncooked portion flow underneath. When egg is set but still moist, remove from heat and fold in half. Slide omelet onto serving platter and top with tomato sauce. Serves 6.

ONION PIE
the flavor of tender, sweet onions is highlighted by melted cheddar cheese

3/4 cup soda cracker crumbs
1/4 cup butter, melted
2 cups thinly sliced onions, separated into rings
2 tablespoons butter or margarine
2 eggs, beaten
3/4 cup milk
1/4 teaspoon salt
dash pepper
1/2 cup shredded cheddar cheese

Combine cracker crumbs with 1/4 cup melted butter. Press crumbs into the bottom and up the sides of an 8 inch pie plate. In a small saucepan, combine onions with 2 tablespoons butter, cover and cook over low heat until onions are soft and transparent. Spoon onions over cracker crust in pie plate. In a small bowl, beat eggs with milk, salt and pepper; pour over onions. Sprinkle cheese over all. Bake in a 350° oven for 30 minutes or until a knife inserted in the center comes out clean. Serves 4.

PEPPERS STUFFED WITH BROWN RICE
a tasty filling of cheese and rice baked in a colorful shell

4 green peppers
3 cups cooked brown rice
2 large tomatoes, chopped
1/2 teaspoon oregano
1/4 teaspoon salt
dash pepper
grated Parmesan cheese

Slice stem ends off peppers, remove seeds and core; steam or parboil peppers for 5 minutes, or just until beginning to soften. Drain and set aside. In a large bowl, combine rice, tomatoes, oregano, salt, pepper and 1/2 cup grated Parmesan cheese. Fill peppers with rice mixture and sprinkle each with additional Parmesan cheese. Place peppers in baking dish, adding water to cover the bottom of dish. Bake at 350° for 20 minutes or until peppers are tender. Serves 4.

JACK CHEESE RATATOUILLE
a savory blend of vegetables topped with melted cheese

1 onion, chopped
2 cloves garlic, minced
2 tablespoons olive oil
1 small eggplant, cubed
1 medium-size zucchini, sliced
1 green pepper, sliced
4 tomatoes, chopped *or* 1 (16 oz.) can tomatoes, chopped, and their liquid
1/2 teaspoon basil
1/4 teaspoon salt
1/4 teaspoon pepper
1 cup shredded Monterey jack cheese

In a large saucepan, sauté onion and garlic in oil. Add eggplant, zucchini, green pepper, tomatoes, basil, salt and pepper. Bring to a boil, reduce heat and simmer for 20 minutes. Remove to serving dish and top with shredded cheese. Serve at once.

SPINACH AND FETA CHEESE BAKE
feta cheese adds a distinctive flavor to spinach

4 cups chopped spinach, firmly packed
1/4 cup chopped green onions
4 eggs, beaten
1 cup crumbled feta cheese
1/2 cup soda cracker crumbs

In a large bowl, combine spinach, green onions, eggs, feta cheese and cracker crumbs. Spoon mixture into a greased 8 by 8 inch pan. Bake, covered, in 350° oven for 30 minutes or until a knife inserted into the center comes out clean. Serves 4.

SUMMER SQUASH CASSEROLE
try a combination of summer squash for a tasty casserole

4 cups cubed zucchini, crookneck or pattypan squash, or a combination
1/2 cup chopped onion
1 cup ricotta cheese
1/4 cup chopped fresh parsley
1 clove garlic, minced
2 eggs, beaten
dash salt
1/2 cup grated Parmesan cheese

In a covered saucepan, boil squash and onion in a small amount of water for 5 minutes or until just tender. Drain thoroughly. In a small bowl, combine ricotta cheese, parsley, garlic, eggs, salt and Parmesan cheese. Stir into squash mixture and place in a greased baking dish. Bake in 350° oven for 30 minutes or until heated through. Serves 6.

STIR-FRY VEGETABLES, TOFU AND RICE
this colorful combination makes a complete meal

1 tablespoon vegetable oil
2 stalks celery, sliced diagonally into 1 inch pieces
3 carrots, sliced diagonally into 1 inch pieces
1-1/2 cups green beans, sliced diagonally into 1 inch pieces
2 tablespoons soy sauce
1 (12 oz.) package tofu (soy bean cake), drained and cut into 1/2 inch cubes
2 green onions, sliced
2 cups cooked brown rice

Heat oil in Chinese wok or skillet and stir-fry celery, carrots and green beans for 5 minutes or until just tender. Remove vegetables from wok and set aside. To wok add soy sauce, tofu and green onions; stir-fry until golden, about 1 minute. Add rice and stir-fry to heat through. Return vegetables to wok and toss with tofu and rice until thoroughly combined. Serves 4.

VEGETABLE STEW
the whole family will enjoy this robust blend of flavors and textures

6 small whole white onions, peeled
3 leeks, sliced*
3 stalks celery, sliced
4 carrots, sliced
2 tablespoons butter or margarine
2 tablespoons all-purpose flour
4 tomatoes, chopped
4 small new potatoes, quartered
1 small head cauliflower, cut into flowerettes
1 cup chicken or vegetable broth
salt
pepper
chopped fresh parsley, for garnish

In a dutch oven, cook onions, leeks, celery and carrots in butter for 15 minutes or until almost tender. Stir in flour and add tomatoes, potatoes, cauliflower pieces and broth. Bring to a boil, cover and simmer for 30 minutes or until vegetables are tender. Season with salt and pepper to taste. Top with parsley. Serves 6.

*To clean leeks thoroughly, cut lengthwise to expose center of stalk. Rinse layers well as needed.

PASTA VEGETABLE TOSS
spinach noodles tossed with broccoli, mushrooms and tomatoes

3 quarts water
1/2 teaspoon salt
1 tablespoon vegetable oil
8 ounces spinach or plain egg noodles
2 tablespoons butter or margarine
2 tablespoons olive oil
1 bunch broccoli, cut into flowerettes and stalks removed
2 cups sliced fresh mushrooms
2 tomatoes, chopped
1 clove garlic, minced
salt
pepper
grated Parmesan cheese

In a large saucepan, bring water to a boil with 1/2 teaspoon salt and 1 tablespoon oil. Add noodles and boil, uncovered, for 8 to 10 minutes or until tender—*al dente*. Drain and toss with butter. While noodles are boiling, heat olive oil in a large skillet. Add broccoli flowerettes and sauté, stirring occasionally, for 5 minutes. Add mushrooms, tomatoes and garlic; sauté an additional 5 minutes, or until vegetables are just tender. Toss with hot buttered noodles and season with salt and pepper to taste. Sprinkle with Parmesan cheese. Serves 4.

ZUCCHINI AND OLIVE FRITTATA
offer brunch guests this unusual dish and you'll catch compliments

2 cups shredded zucchini
2 green onions, sliced
1 clove garlic, minced
1 (2-1/4 oz.) can ripe olives, drained and sliced
1 tablespoon chopped fresh parsley
2 cups shredded cheddar cheese
4 eggs, beaten
salt
pepper

In a large bowl, combine zucchini, green onions, garlic, olives, parsley, cheese, eggs and salt and pepper to taste. Spoon into a greased 8 by 8 inch baking dish. Bake in 350° oven for 30 minutes or until a knife inserted into the center comes out clean. Serves 4.

RECIPE INDEX

Artichoke Quiche, 45
Asparagus Bisque, 17
Asparagus Polanaise, 34
Borscht, 18
Broccoli Soufflé, 46
Brussels Sprouts Parmesan, 36
Butter Sauce, 12
Carrot Rice Casserole, 47
Cauliflower and Walnut Casserole, 48
Cheese Potatoes, 39
Chile Corn Casserole, 50
Cooking Methods, 11
Corn Chowder, 19
Cracked Wheat Cabbage Rolls, 49
Cream of Broccoli Soup, 20
Crudités with Pesto Dip, 32
Eggplant Parmigiana, 51
French Fried Eggplant, 38
Gazpacho Salad, 30
Hollandaise Sauce, 13
Jack Cheese Ratatouille, 55
Mayonnaise, 14
Minestrone, 21
Mushroom Barley Soup, 22
Niçoise Salad, 28
Onion Pie, 53
Orange Glazed Carrots and Onions, 37
Oriental Style Spinach, 44
Pasta Vegetable Toss, 60
Peppers Stuffed with Brown Rice, 54
Potato, Leek and Spinach Soup, 23
Potato Pancakes, 40
Sesame Broccoli Flowerettes, 35
Sherried Sweet Potatoes, 42
Spanish Omelet, 52
Spinach and Feta Cheese Bake, 56
Stir-fry Vegetables, Tofu and Rice, 58
Stuffed Zucchini, 43
Succotash, 41
Summer Squash Casserole, 57
Tangy Artichokes, 33
Tomato Soup, 24
Tomatoes with Avocado Dressing, 31
Tossed Greens with Confetti Dressing, 29
Vegetable Soup, 25
Vegetable Stew, 59
Vegetables, 6-10
Vinaigrette, 16
White Sauce, 15
Winter Squash Soup, 26
Zucchini and Olive Frittata, 61
Zucchini Soup, 27

Owlswood Productions' cookbooks are available at local stores — or directly from the publisher.

Our popular $2.50 series:

___ BUNDT CAKES by Karen Plageman and Susan Herbert
___ THE WOK WAY by Winnie Tuan
___ SLOW-CROCK COOKERY by Karen Plageman
___ THE CREPE BOOK by Susan Herbert
___ BRAVO! ITALIAN COOKING by Cynthia Scheer
___ BAKE BREAD by Marguerite Bencivenga and Barbara Brauer
___ FRENCH COUNTRY FAVORITES by Cynthia Scheer
___ NATURAL FIBER COOKING by Karen Plageman
___ GERMAN HOME COOKING by Cynthia Scheer
___ THE FOOD PROCESSOR BOOK by Pam Biele and Susan Walter
___ THE MICROWAVE WAY by Dorothy McNett
___ GOOD, HEARTY SOUPS by Karen Plageman
___ GREAT CASSEROLES! by Karen Plageman
___ STEAM COOKING NOW! by Barbara Swift Brauer
___ VERSATILE VEGETABLES by Katherine Greenberg and Barbara Kyte

Our Cooking School Series at $5.95:

___ CHINESE COOKING by Mary Wilson
___ MEXICAN COOKING by Cynthia Scheer

Please send me the books indicated above. I enclose my check or money order for _____ books at $2.50 and _____ books at $5.95. I also enclose 75¢ postage and handling. (Calif. residents, add 6% state sales tax.)

NAME_____

ADDRESS_____

CITY, STATE & ZIP CODE_____

Complete and mail to: Owlswood Productions, 1355 Market St., San Francisco, CA 94103.

Please note — prices subject to change without notice.